12/25/09

You make us feel *HAPPY*!
Merry Christmas, Ivy—

Auntie Heather, Uncle Beau,
Emmy & Jake

I ♥ 2

I ♥ GRAMPA ♥

HAPPY. sa silly. mad.

WORLD makesme

feel Irie ♥

09 10 11 12 13 14 PCK 09 08 07 06 05 04 03 02 01

www.accordpublishing.com

ISBN-13: 978-0-7407-8430-9
ISBN-10: 0-7407-8430-7

Library of Congress Control Number: 2009921301

Happy, Sad, silly, Mad
My World Makes Me Feel

written by
John E. Mitchell

illustrated by
Jana Christy

ACCORD PUBLISHING
a division of Andrews McMeel Publishing, LLC
Denver, Colorado

The moon
makes me
curious.

Leaves make

me excited!

Mirrors make me confused.

Mirrors make me
confused.

Goats

Shopping makes **me** angry!

The
beach

make me

embarrassed.

cake

makes

me

ICE makes me

frustrated!

Balloons make me